Praise for *When*

Over the years, Julia ⸺ Duncan has established herself as an acolyte of Appalachia, a daughter of song, with a voice as true as a plumb line, and a capacious gaze that stirs her to unforgettable language. Her latest volume of poetry, *When Time Was Suspended*—a fascinating, richly imagined conflation of history, ethnography, genealogy, ancestry, family Bible, and a suite of ekphrastic masterpieces—only adds to her growing, formidable oeuvre. Duncan's books are dazzling, indisputable knockouts, and this might be her best

—Joseph Bathanti, North Carolina Poet Laureate & Author of *Light at the Seam*

When Time Was Suspended features Julia Nunnally Duncan in full possession of her craft as she renders moments in time with haunting sensitivity, turning sights into insights, sounds into subjects. Nostalgic, prophetic, and profound, these poems of family and place tell aching stories about moments and scenes long gone that, nevertheless, persist.

—Allen Mendenhall, Author of *A Glooming Peace This Morning*

WHEN TIME WAS SUSPENDED

Poems

Julia Nunnally Duncan

REDHAWK
PUBLICATIONS

ISBN: 978-1-959346-37-1 (Paperback)

Library of Congress Control Number: 2024930379

The names and incidents recorded in these poems are based on the author's memories, family stories, and historical photographs. These inclusions are offered with utmost respect and with no harm intended to any person, living or dead.

Front cover image photograph courtesy of Julia Nunnally Duncan.

Book design by Robert T Canipe

Printed in the United States of America.

First printing edition 2024.

Redhawk Publications

The Catawba Valley Community College Press

2550 Hwy 70 SE

Hickory NC 28602

Contents

V

VI

Reflections on Photographs of Nineteenth Century Illness and Death

Reflections on Photographs of the Victims of
Petersburg, American Civil War

For my loved ones today
and for those who shared my yesterdays.

O, call back yesterday, bid time return.

—William Shakespeare, *Richard II*, 3.2

I

Panters

Her grandma called them *panters*
and declared they ran through the mountains.
The girl lay in bed under a patchwork quilt
in the loft of her grandma's house
and listened to the waterfall rushing out back.
But when she fell asleep and dreamed,
she heard the panthers screaming
as they moved stealthily in the woods,
coming closer and closer to her.

Remnants

When Grandma came to the cotton mill village
to visit her daughter's family for a while,
the girl walked with her to town
to shop in the basement of the Belks store.
Town offered so much more
than what her grandma trudged there to find;
yet the girl enjoyed the time they spent together,
Grandma in a dress that hung to her feet
and black lace-up shoes she always wore,
her white hair pinned in a bun.
Never mind the movie theaters,
dime store, and cafes
that on another trip the girl might explore.
Today it was a bag of remnants
they had come for—
cloth scraps of different colors and designs
that Grandma could stitch in a patchwork quilt.

Piggly Wiggly

After a week in the country visiting her cousins,
the girl was ready to go home
to the cotton mill village where her family lived.
Her uncle Manley filled his truck bed with lumber
from his sawmill
to deliver to Broyhill Furniture Factory;
and with her grandma, who lived with Manley,
along for the ride,
the three of them headed to town.
On the way,
they stopped at the Piggly Wiggly
so Grandma could get a slice of cheese
and some crackers to eat.
This was a treat for Grandma
and a habit she always had then,
when they drove into town from the country.

The Accident

Her son Manley found Grandma
lying on the ground underneath the tree limb
that had cracked and come crashing down
upon her shoulder.
She had just carried a bucket
filled with dishes of food
for his dinner at the sawmill—
a hard climb up the ridge to the clearing
from the house where she lived
with Manley's family.
It was a journey she often made at dinnertime.
But this day,
the accident left her lucky to be alive
to face other trials that would come her way.

True Romance

When the woman came home to visit her mama,
she found her grandma sitting on the front porch
in a rocking chair.
"What are you doing, Grandma?" she asked,
noticing a magazine in Grandma's hands.
First thing her grandma did
was reach out to grasp the sleeve of her dress
to feel its material—
something she had always been interested in.
Her sight was weak,
despite her eyeglasses,
and touch was more reliable now.
"Are you reading that magazine?"
the woman asked,
realizing it was a *True Romance*.
"No, I'm just looking at the pictures,"
her grandma said,
as if to hide the truth.
The woman smiled at the idea
of her grandma having a romantic heart—
a side of Grandma she had never seen.

Great-Grandma

For Julia Burgin Ledford (1867-1955)

I may not have inherited your temperament—
yours fiery, mine reserved,
and your eyes were gray
while mine are blue.
but our high cheekbones are the same,
and I can see in your pictures
other features you might have passed down to me.
Though I didn't know you,
I feel like I do
through my mother's vivid memories
that have brought you back to life.
Strange how her recollections
can take me to a time
when you were a part of this world
as I am now.
You lived and loved as I do—
though your life was much harder
than my own.
And you were loved by others in your day.
I wish there were some way,
Great-Grandma,
I could let you know
how much you mean to me, too.

II

Apron

She worked in Clinchfield cotton mill,
and that evening after quitting time,
she filled her apron pockets with rocks
big enough to hold her down
when she walked into the waters of Lake James
to drown.

Image

In the 1930s,
the teenagers happened to be
at Lake James that day
when the drowned man—
a well-known figure in town—
was dragged to the sandy shore.
One of the girls noted
that the body still wore
black shoes and white socks.
The image
would haunt her forever.

Lake Tahoma

He refused to leave his wife;
after all, he was a man well-known
in the community,
and the scandal would be too much to bear.
Yet he couldn't see his way to desert his girlfriend,
whom he cared for dearly.
So with his lover beside him in his car
he drove into Lake Tahoma—
the water taking the two in its embrace
and ensuring he wouldn't have to face
his dilemma anymore.

Mildred

In her parents' house,
near the railroad tracks,
Mildred lay in state
for mourners to come and view her—
her blonde hair spread about her shoulders,
her blue eyes closed forever.
Some remembered the pretty sixteen-year-old
as a clerk in the local Belks store,
but more whispered that day
about the way she couldn't have the married man
so she shot herself instead,
thinking she'd be better off dead
than bereaved of his love.

Oak Tree

The cotton mill families had heard the tale—
as far back as any could recall—
of the lynching at the oak tree
behind the Methodist church.
None knew what the man had done
to be punished this way,
and now a tire swing hung on a stout limb
so children could play there of a day.
But come night they stayed away
for fear they might see the ball of fire
that some claimed would appear
in the darkness at the tree.

Colitis

The diarrhea was virulent,
and his cotton diaper stayed soiled
with a pale stool that seeped through the cloth
and onto the floorboards when he crawled.
Not much anyone could do—
not even the company doctor
who knew the baby wouldn't last long.
They all loved him—
he was such a fair child,
his blond hair and blue eyes
rare amongst his darker siblings.
He was their pet
who would soon become a regret
in all their hearts.
To lose this baby brother and son
at fourteen months old
was a tragedy for the cotton mill family—
hard for anyone to understand
even then in the 1920s
when such misfortune came often
to so many.

Quinsy

The company doctor—
a frequent visitor at the girl's mill village house—
came to lance the abscesses on her swollen tonsils.
It was his remedy to release the pus
so she could swallow and be well again.
But when she saw his familiar coupe
pull up in front of her house,
she wanted to run and hide in the outside toilet
as she had done
that day she fled his office in town
while he prepared for her tonsillectomy.
Horrified of surgery,
she sneaked the two miles home
and hid in the toilet
till he came looking for her
and then gave up and went away.
She was afraid today, too,
of his lancet in her throat.
But she would stay inside the house
and let the doctor do his work.

Rheumatic Fever

It was 1942,
and the baby's fever was so high
his mother wrapped him in wet towels
to try to bring his temperature down.
The fever passed,
yet his mother knew
all was not well with her son.
When he became a toddler,
his eyes—
large and brown—
were set in a guarded stare,
as if he had all the cares of the world
locked in there.
And as he grew,
his words were few and his speech unclear,
and only family knew what he tried to say.
His nerves were frayed,
and when the train rumbled by his house,
he hid under the bed,
where he would stay
until the train was far away.
He lost his father and his mother,
and for the remainder of his life
he lived at one rest home after another.
And so it would be
till he died at sixty-three
from a failed heart as weak as his mind,
both ravaged in that long-ago time
by a fever.

III

The Great War

Yours has the suffering been,
The memory shall be ours.

—Henry Wadsworth Longfellow, "Decoration Day"

It touched the mothers
who mourned their sons
and the wives whose hearts were lonely
and the girls whose marriages
would not come;
and it touched the boys and men
who left them for a cause
that some could not understand
or survive
or recover from.
It touched them all then—
in the glory and regret—
and now this hundred years later
we must never forget.

Christmas Truce, 1914

For some, the sting of savage loss
and brand of old propaganda
were too great to allow them
to let down their guard
and come together in No Man's Land.
Yet for many, the sanctity of Christmas
took away the stigma of *enemy*.
On Christmas Eve, carols could be heard
in the darkness
that was lit by candlelight and moon glow—
"*Stille Nacht, Heilige Nacht* "
and "The First Nowell,"
sung in beautiful, clear voices rising like ghosts
to show the soldiers' hearts longed for home.
So one by one, they ventured out of their trenches
and into a frost-covered territory where bodies lay,
some having stayed there unburied since October.
With shouts of "Merry Christmas!"
the Germans and British shook hands
and shared gifts of cigarettes and little souvenirs
in a place where before none had dared to enter.
Here, for this moment,
they became chums—
Fritz and Tommy—
men weary of war,
happy to be free again
to sing, to applaud, to love,
and not to hate;
to celebrate a time dear to them,
some praying that the truce would continue
into the New Year
and the war be finally over.

Postcard

On the postcard's cover
is a color illustration
of a uniformed soldier and a young nurse.
He stands patiently,
his tunic sleeves pushed up,
while she bandages his left forearm,
his head already bound.
She smiles as she works,
and he smiles, too.
It is a pleasant scene—
no blood to mar its serenity—
one that promises his full recovery.
Below the drawing a caption reads
REPAIRING A MAN OF WAR.

The postcard was stored
with my great-grandmother's things.
I wonder if,
in 1918,
she looked at the image
and thought of her son Condia,
hoping a nurse tended him
in such a caring way
as he lay wounded in France.

Collar Disks

When I was a child,
my grandmother gave two metal disks to me
along with other mementos:
a wedding ring, two thimbles, a pair of spectacles,
and a skeleton key—
items that had belonged to her mother.
For years I kept the disks stored away
until one day I took them out
and looked at them.
One was embellished with a *US*
and the other with crossed cannons
atop the number *89*—
symbols that simply suggested the military.
But then when I came across a portrait
of my great-uncle Charlie,
my grandmother's brother,
I noticed identical insignia—
a *U.S.* and crossed cannons over an *89*—
pinned to the collar of his doughboy tunic.
Suddenly I realized that the metal disks
I'd kept hidden away
were souvenirs of the Great War,
part of a uniform Charlie had worn in France.
That day of my discovery
the disks gained deeper value,
and I was grateful for the gift
that my grandmother had so long ago
bestowed on me.

Jentry's Bullet Pouch

The bullet pouch belonged to a man
I never really knew.
As I child,
I saw Jentry walking up our street,
heading to his house at the top of the hill.
He lived there until he went to Broughton—
a mental hospital—
where he would stay for the rest of his life.
When my cousin's wife settled her parents' estate,
she gave away many of their things—
including the leather pouch—
some to my mother,
who passed them along to me.

Inside the pouch is a single long bullet—
a 30-06, my husband explains,
ammunition that Jentry would have used
in World War I,
his gun a Springfield rifle.
I wonder now if the missing bullets
were spent in battle
and if what he went through in France
had something to do with his mind being lost
in his later years.

It's sobering to think that I,
a stranger to Jentry,
have ended up with his bullet pouch—
something he desperately depended on
when he faced unspeakable danger
a century ago.

November 11, 2018

The bells pealed that Sabbath morning
in our town—
our church bell one of them—
to celebrate the centennial of Armistice Day.
I stepped outside into brisk air to listen
while my fellow congregants stayed inside,
our Eucharist suspended for the moment.
I sent a silent prayer
for those who had fought, suffered, and died.
It was a time of reflection and joy
as it must have been then
when the Great War ended.

IV

Nature

Yesterday I saw a sharp-shinned hawk
grasping a sparrow in its talons
as it flew toward the woods.
The small bird's feathers sprinkled the air
as the hawk carried it away.
Later, my husband explained to me
that the hawk would have eyases
in a nest now
and was taking food to her young.
Yet the image of the bird
trapped in the hawk's clasp
has haunted me
like the memory of the crow
that stole a baby robin from the nest
in our maple tree,
so brazenly carrying the naked creature
through the air
while the parents frantically fluttered about,
chirping in distress.
I watched helpless and horrified
and wanted to kill the crow.
Robert Frost once observed that
nature was cruel,
and when I see the predators around me,
I have to agree.

Poison Oak

When I told my husband
that the poison oak vine—
one I had fought last summer—
was already entwining my dahlia sprout,
he said,
"Poison oak is the Devil of plants"
and quickly added, "and kudzu, too."
We have our share of both demons
on our property—
poison oak taking our hedge
and choking our climbing rose;
and kudzu covering our pasture
and wrapping around our trees.
At least the insidious honeysuckle vine
offers a sweet fragrance to the breeze,
though it's a devil, too, in its way.
Robert Frost said
the woods were all killing each other,
fighting for a place in the sun,
one tree overpowering another
in its shadow.
I witness such struggles every day
and sometimes feel helpless in the foray,
suspecting the poison oak and kudzu
and honeysuckle vine
are trying to get me, too.

Nest

When the workers were here
to trim our hedge and get the weeds
under control,
one of them said,
"I want to show you the yellow jackets' nest
I ran into,"
and he pointed out the hole
where the bees were coming and going
in their frantic way,
and I saw the red, swollen spot on his forearm
where he had been stung.
"They've started again,"
I told my husband,
and we remembered the summer day
when he mowed over a yellow jackets' nest
in our garden
and was stung on his back and chest;
and the way his upper lip and eyelids swelled
and the fast drive to the hospital
where the staff seemed urgent
to keep him alive.
We recalled that catastrophe
and wondered what this summer might bring,
dreading the possibilities.

Bandit

For Steve

He loved his dog Bandit,
and I deem
he sometimes held him in higher esteem
than his daughter or wife.
For Bandit—
wolf-like creature of questionable descent—
was the apple of the man's eye,
the joy of his life.
If the dog wanted to seek shelter from the cold
or relief from the heat,
he would boldly go into the man's workshop
to find a comfortable seat,
no penalty applied.
In fact, the man took great pride
in having the dog so close to him.
Gifts were lavish—
furry squirrel toys and chewy treats
the man bought at Food Lion
and brought home to his pet.
And yet—
Bandit was a sneaky one,
growing more sly and underhanded every day.
Still, the man would let the dog
have his way around the property.
He loved Bandit,
and Bandit loved him.
It was a companionship like no other—
a kind of man-dog brotherhood
that none but the two of them understood.

Copperhead

The copperhead appeared early that year
on an evening in June,
coiled up in our driveway,
alarmingly close to the house.
We heard our border collie Bandit
barking frantically
and knew by his tone
that he was on a snake.
He had it cornered,
and when it struck at him,
he snapped at it,
grabbing it in his mouth
and shaking it furiously.
He flung it across the driveway
and then carried it into our yard,
while I screamed for him to leave it alone,
knowing he had been bit.
I finally coaxed him away from the snake
so my husband could shoot it
with his revolver,
and then I picked up the body
with a long stick
and carried it to the creek
where I threw it in.
Bandit survived the ordeal,
though I knew he would face another snake,
another day.

A Good Dog

He was a snake fighter as a puppy,
grabbing a king snake from our dirt basement
and running with it into the yard.
So I might have expected his fate
ten years later.
That July night
when I heard Bandit's frantic barking,
I knew what I would find when I went outside.
Bandit had it trapped against the house,
where it was coiled and striking.
I took a stick and bashed its head
and threw its body into the creek,
knowing it had bitten Bandit repeatedly.
For a week my family nursed him,
thinking we could get him through
(as we knew he had survived
copperhead bites before).
But our efforts were in vain.
Too sick to eat,
one evening he offered his paw to me,
gazing at my face solemnly,
as if he were saying goodbye.
We found him the next morning
and buried him in our backyard,
where I place flowers at his grave to honor him—
a good dog, dear friend, loyal to the end.

In Winter

In winter,
the icy air and falling snow
drive me inside my home
to hide in the warmth
of a wood fire's embrace,
soft lamplight encasing me
in its glow.
A book for company,
I seek comfort in my solitude,
retreating from the hard months
of planting and growing
and harvesting and preserving
my garden's bounty.
Winter for me
is freedom and a patient wait
for the spring to bring back labor
that the earth requires.
In winter,
I find solace and a quieter mind—
a stillness
and time of rest and renewal.

Seedlings

My Campari seeds,
retrieved from store-bought tomatoes,
were planted in rich soil,
side-by-side in seed starter pots
to rest in a sunny spot in my house.
Through the last cold weeks of winter
the seeds persevered
till tiny green shoots appeared,
promising hearty transplants
for my garden plot.
But on this mid-March day,
as my seedlings sunned on the patio table,
a wayward wind blew
and lifted the peat pot tray,
dumping the new shoots and soil
in the grass nearby.
Appalled, I gathered what limp seedlings
I could find
and replanted them in a studier vessel outside.
Whether they revive in the soil
and thrive during the spring
I won't know for a while.
But there's always hope
in gardening.

V

Christmas Eve in 1964

My brother Steve and I couldn't sleep
that Christmas Eve in 1964.
We lay in bed
and whispered and waited
till he said, "I think he's here!"
and I hissed, "Listen!"
while my heart pounded in the dark.
I had written to Santa,
asking for a desk and chair
and a View-Master Theater,
declaring that I had been very good,
helping my mother wash dishes
and carrying in wood for our cook stove.
When we heard the cuckoo clock in the front room
sound three *cuckoo*s,
we knew we couldn't wait any longer,
so our bare feet hit the floor.
After all, Santa had come and gone already
and left our treasures just down the hall
under our tinsel-covered Christmas tree.

My Grandmother's Bedtime

It was my grandmother's bedtime,
though dusk had scarcely fallen
and twilight seeped through
her lace curtains.
I lay quiet beside her,
sunk in the billowy feather mattress,
not daring to move
for fear I'd injure her frail body.
My heart heavy,
I could barely keep from crying.
It was my night to keep her company,
but I longed to be home,
playing hide-and-seek with friends outside
or watching TV with my family.

My Father's Barbecue Ribs

On summer days,
a savory scent wafted from our backyard
when my father lifted the lid of the barbecue grill.
His spare ribs were the highlight of our cookouts—
boiled beforehand by my mother
so that when he grilled them,
brushing on a sauce, tangy and sweet,
the meat would be tender and juicy.
Nothing fancy then in the 1960s—
no television cooking shows
with restaurateurs to instruct you
on the secrets of perfect barbecue—
just a simple charcoal grill,
a mother's preparation,
and a father's skill
in making the tastiest pork ribs imaginable.

That Tuesday Morning

I thought we lived in Mayberry—
our town as quiet and friendly and safe—
and Western North Carolina seemed a world away
from New York City.
Yet it didn't seem so distant
that Tuesday morning in September
when the horror filled our TV screens
and started our telephones ringing
with the news.
My mother called and said,
"Did you see what happened?"
and I could hear the fear in her voice.
"Where will they hit next?" we wondered
and found ourselves looking at the sky.
My community college students
were agitated that night,
thinking we might be targeted.
I was grateful for the normality of work that day,
but hesitant to be away from my husband and baby.
The world changed that Tuesday morning—
our security and complacency gone.
Suddenly Mayberry was an illusion,
and we couldn't see how life
would ever be the same.

Dream

In my dream
she is a baby still,
cradled in my arms,
sheltered from any harm
that might come her way.
As I hold her,
she looks up at me,
and I can see
she feels the depth of my love—
never wavering,
ever constant.
But in reality,
she is twenty now
and has left me behind
to find a life,
a purpose of her own.
And I am left to dream,
as mothers do,
of a time when I was her world
and she was mine.

Together

On that summer day
my daughter and I lay in the yard
and looked up at the passing clouds.
A neighbor drove by and stopped to say
I should be in the house,
working on a novel,
(for she had liked the one I'd written before).
No, I told her,
it was more important to stay where I was.
I knew then that the time would be brief
when my daughter would care
to lie outside with me and look at the sky.
Now, how I wish there had been more such days
when we lay in the grass
or played Frisbee in the yard
or did nothing but simply be together.

My Brother's Garden

How quicky grass covered the plot
where my brother's garden grew,
one he nurtured caringly.
He shared with me some of his bounty—
messes of Blue Lake bush beans,
golden ears of Kandy Korn,
bags of Clemson Spineless okra;
cabbages, tomatoes, cucumbers, peppers—
the harvest of his hard work.
In his final garden,
he grew only a few tomatoes.
I should have known then
that something was wrong.
Now that he is gone,
I see the grassy field and remember him
laboring in the sun:
tilling, hoeing, and lifting his baseball cap
to wipe the sweat from his brow,
resting a moment to survey his work,
knowing he had done it well.

Tabloids

The woman,
whom I had known years before,
accosted me in the grocery store
when she noticed the tabloids
I carried to the checkout lane.
They were for my mother,
who liked reading about the Royal Family
and Hollywood celebrities
and enjoyed working the puzzles inside;
and I loved buying them for her—
a Friday treat
that she looked forward to all week.
The woman said, appalled,
"I can't believe you read that trash!
I'm disappointed in you."
(I had been her English teacher—
someone who, I guess,
wasn't supposed to read something so low.)
Though her criticism was flung at me,
I sensed an insult to my mother's dignity
and told the woman
she should read the tabloids, too,
and learn something she didn't know.
I burst her bubble that day in the grocery store,
dashing any illusions she had about me.
But I didn't want her respect anymore.

We Hoped

We hoped we would be
with our mother again,
sitting in her cozy front room,
hearing stories of the past—
tales familiar and dear.
But her fall
and the hospital stay alone
and then months in the nursing home
when we were kept away
except for brief visits
through a picture window,
conversing on a cell phone,
changed everything.
We prayed we would be
with our mother again—
just to hold her hand
and keep her company.
Surely, the pandemic would end
and the social distancing
that forced us apart.
But it wasn't to be,
and now she is gone,
leaving us with only memories
and broken hearts.

Bobby Pins

My mother rolled her hair with bobby pins
in tight little pin curls that covered her head—
a nightly ritual before she went to bed.
When I found the box of bobby pins
sitting at the back of her dresser,
all those years I had watched her roll her hair
came back to me,
and I grieved I would never see
her do this again.

Wallpaper

How easily my nephew peeled
the gold damask wallpaper
from the front room walls of my mother's house—
like sheets of shedding skin—
to reveal an older wallpaper
that had been hidden underneath.
How many years had I lived within those walls,
watching television with my family
or sitting spellbound under our Christmas tree,
taking for granted the familiar wallpaper
that surrounded me?
In pictures of my sixth birthday party,
my guests and I dance the twist
on the front room's hardwood floor,
the pink floral-patterned wallpaper our backdrop.
To see that wallpaper again
for the first time since childhood
was like reuniting with an old friend.
It, too, would be gone soon,
the walls replaced for a new family.
But the long-ago wallpaper remains with me,
safe in my memory.

Our Old World

Every day we say,
This pandemic will pass
as we try to evade a catastrophe
that has made our lives chaotic.
We will be all right,
we declare,
though hardship and despair
surround us.
No one can tell
when this pestilence will end,
yet we fight,
hoping to win
and get our old world back again.

Photography takes an instant out of time,
altering life by holding it still.

—Dorothea Lange

:

VI

When Time Was Suspended

Mysteries are there—
faces from long ago
that no one today can identify;
and revelations, too—
youthful versions of loved ones
who lived in a past
we never knew.
Photographs capture times
we might forget
if not for an image to remind us
of that day.
Sad, enlightening, and dear
family pictures can be,
allowing us to see
what we and others were then
at that moment
when time was suspended.

Family Portrait

In the family portrait,
my great-grandma Ledford sits in a chair
in front of her eight children.
Her white hair pinned in a bun,
she wears a long cotton dress and apron,
her worn black shoes in shadow,
her walking cane lying at her feet.
Her shoulders are slumped
as if they carry the weight
of all the years she's seen.
Four sons stand behind her,
solemn-faced, hats in hand,
her four daughters pressed between them,
their expressions just as somber.
Their demeanor captures the hard life
that they lived back then
when misfortune never seemed far away.
But they were a rough-hewn bunch,
accustomed to toil and survival day-to-day.
Their progeny might have prospered
and been granted a life easier
than they were allowed.
But they were the rich soil
from which the rest of us sprang—
a tough stock,
worthy and proud.

If He Had Come Home

She was to marry him,
and while he was far away,
she dreamed of the day they would wed.
But it was not to be;
killed in France,
he lost his life and their joy over there,
and she cared nothing for marriage any more.
In a portrait of my great-aunt Lola—
made a decade after the war—
she is a stylish woman
in a fur-trimmed coat and cloche hat.
And her dark hair and large brown eyes
reveal the beauty he must have seen.
Yet the solemn expression on her face
shows no trace of happiness.
I wonder if when she heard the news,
she imagined him entangled in barbed wire
in No Man's Land
or lying blood-drained in the mud.
Of course, she couldn't have known
the circumstances of that place,
and her ignorance was a blessing.
She outlived the tragedy seventy years,
existing in a world without him.
But I feel she still dreamed
of how different her life could have been
if he had come home from the war.

Doughboy

In my great-uncle Charlie's portrait,
he wears his doughboy uniform,
and I see the pride he felt then.
He couldn't yet know
that the muddy trenches of France,
stained with the blood of infantrymen,
would be so unlike his peaceful valley
in East Tennessee;
and he couldn't foretell
that the scars he would carry inside
from that distant place
would haunt him till the day he died.
In the portrait of my great-uncle Charlie,
made before he went to war,
his face is eager and his mind unmarred,
his heart set on being part of something grand
and darker than he could imagine.

The Portrait

My father gave the portrait to me,
in fact insisted that I take it
as if he knew it would be
safe in my care.
It is an image of a grandfather
I never knew,
who died too soon after I was born.
Little remained of him in my grandmother's house
other than a walking cane,
a few straight razors,
and the portrait stored upstairs.
The comely young man pictured there
has neatly parted, short dark hair
and wears the Victorian fashion of the day,
with his black dress coat and bow tie
atop a white shirt and high wing collar.
The photograph was taken
before my grandmother's time with him,
when, perhaps, he was loved by the girl
who would become his first wife
and die at twenty-nine,
to be left behind in a cemetery in Tennessee
when he moved away with his new family.
A solemn face gazes from the portrait
that hangs on my guest bedroom wall.
I study it as I polish the gilt-edged frame
and clean the antique glass,
preserving something of my grandfather's past
that has been entrusted to me.

Tennessee Baptism, 1915

In the black-and-white photograph,
my grandfather, in striped shirt and suspenders,
stands in the muddy river,
water soaking his thighs.
His left hand grips the woman's clasped hands,
and his right hand is uplifted;
eyes closed, he prays to the blackening sky.
His congregation waits on the bank:
women, in long skirts and boots,
hold black umbrellas;
men, arms crossed and heads bent
beneath broad-brimmed hats,
Sunday best,
wait for the storm to pass.
And children watch, too:
boys in overalls and floppy hats sit barefoot
on the riverbank
while girls in white dresses and oversized hats
peer around their mothers.
All are gathered to see
the dark-haired woman,
whose head is bowed,
eyes closed,
who waits for the preacher's hand
to cover her mouth and nose—
the quick, wet immersion,
the washing of her soul.

A Reminder

In my late grandmother's things,
stored in a chest of drawers,
I found a handmade oak picture frame
that displayed a floral still life scene—
a magazine clipping she'd framed
in the past.
When I removed the glass pane
and the clipping inside,
I discovered a cabinet card—
a sepia-toned portrait of my grandparents,
a young couple then in Tennessee,
she in Edwardian dress,
he in black suit,
standing with their four children—
a tableau of 1916.

Today I keep the portrait
displayed in the homemade frame—
a reminder of a lost time
and a family in its early days
before more children,
including my father,
had come along
and when decades of life
still lay ahead.

Reflections on Photographs
of Nineteenth Century Illness and Death

James Samuel How, M.D.—
Dead from Cholera Epidemic May 1849

He is a handsome man of twenty-two,
whose thick dark hair,
parted in the middle,
and light beard curling on his white collar
follow the style of the day.
One might say he looks like someone napping:
his head rests on a pillow,
his dark-lashed eyes are closed,
and his lips are opened slightly
as if he breathes peacefully.
From his smooth, unscathed face,
one might conclude he didn't suffer
though this notion would be absurd—
for to have cholera then
meant a horrendous struggle
with vomiting, diarrhea, and asphyxiation—
a wretched end.
It was his effort to heal his patients
that sent him to his premature grave,
his life sacrificed
to save others.

Mother with Child, Dead from Measles
Circa 1857

The mother gazes beyond her child
who rests in her arms, dressed in a burial gown.
The woman's eyes are wet with tears,
and her mouth is drawn down.
Although her white lace collar
and bright earrings and brooch
bring lightness to the image,
and the rose tint on her cheeks
and those of her child
might beguile one to think that
they share good health and vitality,
all that I see
in this mother with her child
is despair.

Young Girl on Patchwork Quilt,
Waterfall Background Circa 1878

The patchwork quilt
that the girl is laid out on
is made of hand-stitched cloth remnants,
light and dark,
with flowers embroidered on its uneven squares.
it could be a quilt that covered her bed
and kept her warm on a winter night.
And the daisy held in her pale fingers
might be like one she picked on a summer day.
This dark-haired rural girl,
who wears a white gown and slippers,
appears simply to be sleeping comfortably
on her homemade patchwork quilt.
Yet this is an illusion built of
suffering and loss.

Woman with Black Smallpox
Six Hours Before Death 1881

The elderly woman's head rests upon
her deathbed pillow.
Her eyes are tightly closed,
and her nostrils and opened mouth
are crusted with the dark blood
that has filled her lungs.
She is dying from a savage form of smallpox,
a disease almost forgotten now.
She could be someone's grandmother,
her fair face etched by age and
her gray hair in disarray
as she lies in her final day of life.
How cruel of this disease
to make her and so many others
suffer this way.

Three Brothers Dead from Infection
1883

Three boys lie side by side,
attired in homely woolen suits.
Their hands, fingers interlaced,
are placed on their bellies,
and their heads, which rest upon a dark pillow,
lean toward each other
as if they share a bed.
These brothers seem to be close in age,
though the middle one is slightly bigger,
and they are still at a stage
when boys play together.
Yet I suspect they were hard workers—
as children then were expected to be—
helpmates stolen from a family
shattered at losing all three.

President Ulysses S. Grant Three Days Before
Death from Throat Cancer July 20, 1885

Maybe because he was a skilled horseman
or that he loved his wife, Julia, so dearly
or that his last name was the same
as that of my great-great grandfather
Samuel Bruce Grant,
who also fought in the Civil War,
though on the opposing side—
maybe these are reasons why
I have looked at Ulysses S. Grant
not as an enemy of my Southern ancestors,
but as possible distant kin.
In the photograph
he sits in a rocking chair
on the front porch of his country home,
and he is surrounded by family.
His shoulders are draped in a shawl,
his face looks pale and gaunt,
and his beard has grown gray;
but his shiny top hat
seems a fashionable affront to the disease
that will soon take him away.
While the young girls in the picture look bored,
the women smile lightly,
as if to add an impression of gaiety to the scene.
But it is in Grant's face—
his weary expression—
that I glean the truth.

Gangrene of the Legs as a Complication
of Diphtheria Circa 1892

The child lies on a bed,
and his bare legs,
black to the knees,
are propped up by a pillow,
so one can clearly see
the progress of the disease.
His hands clutch the top of a blanket
that is folded back to expose his legs,
and his head is just beyond
the picture's edge.
Though the child's face is hidden,
I believe this is a boy who grasps the cloth
with hands that in a better day
might have picked up a stone to throw
or gripped a fishing pole.
I wish there were someway
I could go back in time
and hold this boy's hands in mine,
like a mother would her son's,
and press his small fingers in my clasp.
I would offer solace to him through my company
and pray that he would not suffer
another day.

Reflections on Photographs of the Victims of Petersburg, American Civil War

R. Dillon
2 Battery VRC

This soldier is older than some
who fought at Petersburg.
He has a broad brow, receding hairline,
and dark eyes that glitter like shards of black glass,
as emotionless as he must have felt
when he posed with the chalk board
that identified him.
In the medical photograph,
the white stump that was his right leg
displays itself on the stool seat
under the chalk board,
and the other leg is splayed
as if to get out of the way.
He has done his duty,
sacrificing a part of himself
for a dream of victory
that carried a dear price.

E.O. Van Valkenburgh
CO C 39 IL

The man's eyes are wide-open and wild
as he stares ahead,
posed in semi-profile by the photographer.
His right arm, amputated at the shoulder,
is not in view,
but the wound on the left side of his scalp
where a conoidal ball laid bare his skull
is clear and portends his future
at Kansas State Insane Asylum.
There he will be delusional and suicidal,
still suffering the catastrophe of war.

C.J. Sargent
CO C 1 ME HA

This young boy from Maine
has a fair face unmarred by age or regret.
And yet he has lost his right arm,
now a mangled-looking stump,
from a gunshot wound to the elbow.
Seated on a stool,
he looks up at the photographer—
as he has been instructed to do—
with pale blue, deep-set eyes.
I wonder what he will tell his mother
when he sees her.
Will he apologize to his father
for not coming home whole?
Will he hide his injury from others
and keep his precocious memories
locked inside?

David R. Templeton
CO A 46 NY

Just admitted to the U.S. Army Hospital,
the sixteen-year-old boy seems
barely able to sit for the photographer.
A chalk board with inscription of his name
and the New York company he has served in
is propped up against him,
his tan hands limp in his lap.
Looking fresh from the battlefield,
he has a blood-stained face;
his eyes are closed—
the left one grotesquely swollen—
and his mouth gapes.
In a gunshot wound to the head,
his eyeball has been grazed.
A patient for two months,
he is finally pronounced "well,"
and a new carte de visite is made.
Though his surgeon believes
he is ready to leave the hospital,
the second photograph shows
his left eye still closed—
its sight gone forever—
and his indignation is evident
in the expression on his face.

C. Gillespie
CO F 94 NY

This New York soldier,
a handsome man
with thick dark hair and curly beard,
holds his identification chalk board
with perhaps some chagrin.
Seated on a stool,
he crosses his left leg
to show his amputated foot—
a part of himself lost
to an accidental gunshot wound.
It might be he feels no sense of nobility
in his sacrifice,
but his loss is still great,
and he will suffer its weight
the rest of his life.

George Garrison
CO A 95 NY

The boy in a profile pose
has an upturned nose
and a face speckled with
adolescent acne and freckles.
His jacket tail is lifted to show
a wound on his left side
where a minie ball exited,
fracturing a pelvic bone.
This gunshot injury,
followed by gangrene,
must have caused him
great suffering.
And his aloof expression
suggests he is quite weary
of this adult business of war.

SGT. Martin Burke
CO K 15 NY HA

At twenty-nine,
the New York sergeant
probably felt the press of time
even before the gunshot wound to his left arm
propelled him into a medical Hell
of gangrene, amputation, bone necrosis,
and infection
that must have seemed relentless.
He appears placid enough
in the medical photograph.
Naked to the waist,
he braces his identification board
with his remaining right hand.
His dark hair and beard are well-kempt
and his face attractive.
Still, the scar that runs down his left side
and the stump that hangs from his shoulder
won't allow him to hide
the suffering he has lived with
since his injury.

Michael Serabatsky
CO B 183 PA

The immigrant from Poland
has disheveled dark hair
and stark blue eyes
that stare at the photographer.
His identifying chalk board
is braced in his hands
and propped on his lap,
the right leg of his trousers pulled back
to expose his healing stump.
How does he feel to be so far away
from his native land?
Will he ever understand
the war he has fought in
or why he had to relinquish a limb
for his new country?
He is a man displaced
and bewildered—
the chaos of war
revealed in his face.

Edward Estell
CO B 207 PA

This Pennsylvania soldier's face
exudes anger.
His eyebrows are knitted,
and his mouth is set hard
as if he defies his enemy
whose bullet caused an injury
to his left arm
and a subsequent amputation
so near the joint
that he will never be able to wear
an artificial limb.
Such an indignity for him
is irreconcilable.

Acknowledgments

I gratefully acknowledge the following journals
and anthologies that originally published my poems,
sometimes in slightly different form:

Germ Magazine: "*Panters*" and "Dream"

Evening Street Review: "Remnants,"
"The Accident," and "*True Romance*"

Southern Roots Magazine: "Piggly Wiggly,"
"Great-Grandma," and "Family Portrait"

Speckled Trout Review: "Apron"

Still: The Journal: "Lake Tahoma," "Mildred,"
"Oak Tree," and "Doughboy"

Broad River Review: "Colitis"

Red Dirt Forum: "The Great War," "Christmas
Truce, 1914," and "Postcard"

BlazeVOX online journal: "Collar Disks,"
"Jentry's Bullet Pouch," "November 11, 2018,"
"In Winter," "My Brother's Garden," and "Tabloids"

Critter Absurd: "Bandit"

Crossing the Rift: "That Tuesday Morning"

Everything Is Fine Zine: "Our Old World"

"The Portrait" and the seven poems in **Reflections on Photographs of Nineteenth Century Illness and Death** originally appeared in my collection *A Part of Me* (Red Dirt Press, 2017) and are reprinted with permission of Red Dirt Press.

"Tennessee Baptism, 1915" originally appeared in my collection *An Endless Tapestry* (March Street Press, 2007).

The nine poems in **Reflections on Photographs of the Victims of Petersburg, American Civil War** originally appeared in my collection *A Neighborhood Changes* (Finishing Line Press, 2018) and are reprinted with permission of Finishing Line Press.

I would like to offer my sincere appreciation to Stanley B. Burns, MD, FACS, for granting me permission to use specific titles of photographs collected in the following books:

James Samuel How, M.D.—Dead from Cholera Epidemic May 1849
Mother with Child, Dead from Measles Circa 1857
Young Girl on Patchwork Quilt, Waterfall Background Circa 1878
Three Brothers Dead from Infection 1883
from
Burns, Stanley B., and Elizabeth Burns. *Sleeping Beauty II: Grief, Bereavement and the Family in Memorial Photography: American & European Traditions.* New York: Burns Archive Press, 2002. Print.

*Woman with Black Smallpox Six Hours Before
Death 1881*
*President Ulysses S. Grant Three Days Before
Death from Throat Cancer July 20, 1885*
*Gangrene of the Legs as a Complication of
Diphtheria Circa 1892*
from
Burns, Stanley B. *Respiratory Disease: A
Photographic History 1871-1895: The Antiseptic Era:
Selections from the Burns Archive*. New York: Burns Archive
Press, 2003. Print.

And I would also like to thank Dr. Stanley B. Burns
for granting me permission to use specific titles of
photographs collected in the following book:
*R. Dillon 2 Battery VRC; E.O. Van Valkenburgh
CO C 39 IL; C.J. Sargent CO C 1 ME HA; David R.
Templeton CO A 46 NY; C. Gillespie CO F 94 NY;
George Garrison CO A 95 NY; SGT. Martin Burke CO K 15 NY
HA; Michael Serabatsky CO B 183 PA; Edward Estell CO B 207
PA*
from
Burns, Stanley B. *Shooting Soldiers: Civil War Medical
Photography by R. B. Bontecou*. New York: The Burns
Archive Press, 2011. Print.

About the Author

 Julia Nunnally Duncan is an award-winning author of eleven books of prose and poetry, including a new essay collection *All We Have Loved* (Finishing Line Press, 2023). Her upbringing in a Western North Carolina textile town plays predominantly in her work, which is filled with family, community, and history. An alumnus of Warren Wilson College, Julia taught English and Humanities at McDowell Technical Community College for over thirty years. She now devotes her creative energies to writing and playing classical piano. She lives in Marion, NC, with her husband, Steve, a mountain woodcarver, and enjoys spending time with him and their daughter, Annie.

Made in the USA
Columbia, SC
11 February 2024

31274011R00059